The Saguaro Cactus

by J. Hernandez

Glenview, Illinois • Boston, Massachusetts • Chandler, Arizona
Upper Saddle River, New Jersey

A saguaro cactus

The saguaro cactus is a plant. The saguaro grows in the desert. Some saguaros grow as tall as houses. It takes many years for a saguaro to grow so tall.

A saguaro full of water

The desert is a hot, dry place. The saguaro can live in the desert because it holds water in its body. The saguaro looks fat when it has a lot of water inside. It looks thin when it has less water.

branches

Young saguaros are small.

This saguaro has branches that look like arms.

The saguaro starts as a seed. The seed grows to become a small cactus. The small cactus grows to become a tall, straight cactus. Finally, the tall saguaro grows branches that look like arms.

The flowers of a saguaro cactus

The saguaro cactus grows flowers. The flowers turn into fruit. Like all fruit, cactus fruit has seeds. The seeds from some of that fruit will grow into new saguaros.

spines

The saguaro is covered with sharp, pointy spines. The spines keep some animals from eating the saguaro and its fruit. When it rains, the spines help water go down to the roots of the cactus.

The roots of a saguaro

A saguaro's roots are not deep in the ground. They are spread out near the top of the ground. That way, they can get a lot of water when it rains.

This bird lives in a saguaro.

Many small animals use the saguaro. Birds build nests in holes in the cactus. Bugs eat its seeds and other parts of the plant. Bats get food from the flowers. The saguaro helps all of these animals live.